Hidden Forces of the Universe:
The Secrets of the Spirit World

The Mystical Powers of the Psychic Mind and the Hidden Forces of Intuition, Karma, and Astral Travel That Can Change Your Life Forever

By

Jack Michael

Jack Michael

Copyright © 2025 Jack Michael

All rights reserved.

Jack Michael

DEDICATION

This book is dedicated to all the curious souls who dare to look beyond the physical world, seeking to understand the unseen forces that shape our lives. To those who are ready to embrace the mysteries of the spirit world, trusting in their intuition and the power of energy that surrounds us all. May this work ignite your own spiritual journey and guide you to a life of profound transformation and enlightenment.

Jack Michael

ACKNOWLEDGMENTS

I would like to express my heartfelt gratitude to the incredible souls who have helped bring this book to life. Thank you to my mentors, guides, and spiritual teachers who have shared their wisdom and experiences. Your insight and encouragement have been invaluable. I am deeply grateful to my friends, family, and supporters for their unwavering belief in me. Finally, thank you to every reader who has been curious enough to embark on this mystical journey with me.

Jack Michael

TABLE OF CONTENTS

DEDICATION 3

ACKNOWLEDGMENTS 4

TABLE OF CONTENTS 5

INTRODUCTION 6

CHAPTER 1 9

Unveiling the Spirit World 9

CHAPTER 2 16

The Psychic Mind and Intuition 16

CHAPTER 3 24

The Mystical Powers of Karma 24

CHAPTER 4 32

Astral Travel – A Gateway to Other Realms 32

CHAPTER 5 45

The Hidden Forces That Shape Our Lives 45

CHAPTER 6 57

Facing the Dark Forces – Protection from Negative Entities . 57

CHAPTER 7 65

Transforming Your Life with Mystical Knowledge 65

CHAPTER 8 81

Embracing the Mystical Path 81

CONCLUSION 88

INTRODUCTION

Imagine, for a moment, that the universe you see with your eyes—the one filled with stars, mountains, oceans, and cities—is just the surface. Beneath it all, there lies a hidden realm, a universe of unseen energies, forces, and spirits silently guiding everything you know. These forces—mystical, powerful, and often elusive—hold the key to unlocking your deepest desires, fears, and purpose. They are the architects of your soul's journey, and yet, they remain invisible to most.

What if I told you that you have the power to tap into this unseen world? That you can access a hidden dimension of intuition, karma, and astral travel? That within you lies the ability to understand the very forces that shape not only your life but the universe itself?

This book will take you on an extraordinary journey—one that dives deep into the spirit world, where secrets of the psychic mind, the laws of karma, and the incredible power of astral travel await to be uncovered. Here, you will explore the mystical forces that influence your every move, choice, and experience. These forces have been quietly at work in your life, shaping your destiny in ways you may never have imagined.

But why now? Why should you open yourself to these hidden realms? The world as we know it is changing, and the pursuit of spiritual wisdom is no longer a luxury; it is a necessity. Whether you are looking for answers to life's deepest questions, seeking personal transformation, or simply yearning to understand the mysteries that surround us, the time to tap into the hidden forces of the universe is now.

Throughout these pages, you will uncover ancient wisdom and modern practices that will empower you to connect with the spirit world like never before. You will learn how to open your third eye, master the energies around you, and transform your life in ways you never thought possible. It's not just about seeing what's hidden—it's about awakening to the truth of who you really are.

By the time you finish reading, you won't just believe in the unseen; you'll become a part of it. You'll experience the undeniable power that comes with understanding your intuition, navigating the currents of karma, and mastering the art of astral travel. These hidden forces are not mere fantasy or wishful thinking—they are real, they are powerful, and they are waiting for you to unlock them.

Are you ready to step into the unknown? The journey begins now.

CHAPTER 1

Unveiling the Spirit World

As the first light of dawn breaks over the horizon, we may look out into the world and see only the physical: trees swaying in the breeze, the soft glow of the sun, and the bustling energy of life. But what if I told you that there is so much more to this world than meets the eye? A hidden realm that exists just beyond the physical, a place where energies, spirits, and forces silently interact with the lives we lead. This realm is known as the spirit world—a dimension that exists alongside our own, influencing everything from our relationships to the very course of our destiny.

The spirit world is not some distant, ethereal place beyond the stars. It is here, in the spaces between breaths, in the energy fields that surround us. The air we breathe is infused with energies that carry memories, intentions, and vibrations from all that has come before. Imagine this realm as a vast network of souls, energies, and entities—an unseen web that connects every life, every moment, every experience. While we cannot always see it with our eyes, the spirit world is always there, influencing us in ways we cannot always comprehend.

It is said that the spirit world does not merely exist in isolation, but interacts with our lives in subtle, profound ways. From the moment we are born to the day we depart this world, we are guided by spirits—both benevolent and malevolent—that leave their mark on our journey. Benevolent spirits, or guides, watch over us, offering wisdom, protection, and insight. They are the silent teachers that nudge us in the right direction, guiding us toward our higher purpose. Then there are the malevolent spirits, energies that seek to disrupt our peace, sow confusion, or even manipulate our actions. These dark forces often work through the very vulnerabilities we carry—fear, anger, doubt—feeding off the negative energies we allow to dominate our lives. The spirit world, therefore, is not just a place of peace and love, but also a battleground, where light and dark vie for control over our souls.

And yet, despite the powerful presence of the spirit world, most of us remain unaware of its influence. We go about our daily lives, unaware of the subtle currents that guide us, protect us, and challenge us. So, how can we access this hidden realm? How can we see the unseen?

The answer lies in the third eye—a mystical, powerful center of perception that opens the door between the physical world and the spiritual realm. Often referred to as the "inner eye," the third eye is believed to be a gateway to higher consciousness, intuition, and psychic abilities. It is not a physical eye, but rather an energetic center located in the middle of the forehead, between the eyebrows. When awakened, the third eye grants access to visions, deeper understanding, and the ability to perceive energies and spirits beyond the ordinary. It is through this center that we can begin to see what lies hidden—whether it be the benevolent guides offering us their wisdom or the darker forces seeking to manipulate us.

Many people who have experienced the opening of their third eye speak of the profound transformations that follow. For some, it may begin with a sudden awareness—a feeling of being connected to something greater, a surge of energy that flows through their being. Others experience vivid dreams, flashes of insight, or encounters with entities from the spirit world. In my own life, the awakening of my third eye was not a gentle process. It came with startling clarity, as if a veil had been lifted, revealing a world of spirits and energies that I had never seen before. I recall one night, waking up in the stillness of my home, only to find myself face to face with a spirit—an entity whose presence was so powerful that it left me breathless. It wasn't a ghost in the traditional sense—there were no chains, no floating apparitions—but a being of pure energy, sitting before me, eyes locked with mine. And in that moment, I knew: I had crossed over into a realm that was always there but had remained hidden from me.

This experience, like so many others, was only possible because of the activation of the third eye. Through it, I was able to see what had been hidden, to sense the energies that moved between the worlds. But this power comes with responsibility, for the third eye reveals not only the peaceful forces that guide us, but also the darker entities that seek to distort our paths. It is a tool that must be used with caution, for once the veil is lifted, there is no going back.

For many, the process of awakening the third eye can be a gradual one. It may begin with small signs: intuitive insights, strange dreams, or a sense that something more is at play in our lives. With practice, these experiences grow stronger, and our connection to the spirit world deepens. It is through this awakening that we gain the ability to navigate the spirit world with greater awareness, to distinguish between the benevolent forces that seek our growth and the darker energies that threaten to lead us astray.

The spirit world is not a place of mere fantasy; it is a realm of real power, real influence, and real beings. From the moment we tap into the energy of our third eye, we begin a journey that will change the way we perceive ourselves and the world around us. The question is not whether you are ready to see the unseen; the question is whether you are willing to embrace the truths that lie beyond the veil.

As you continue reading, I invite you to open your heart, open your mind, and awaken your third eye. For once you begin to see the hidden forces that shape your life, there is no turning back. The spirit world is waiting for you to discover its secrets. Will you answer the call?

CHAPTER 2

The Psychic Mind and Intuition

The human mind is a remarkable entity, capable of both conscious reasoning and a deeper, more mysterious form of perception. While we may pride ourselves on our logical minds, we often overlook the profound power of our psychic mind—the part of us that connects to a higher state of awareness, linking us directly to the soul. This aspect of our mind goes beyond the physical senses, tapping into a dimension where energy, emotions, and unseen forces interact with us on a constant basis. The psychic mind is not something supernatural or far-fetched; it is simply the part of our being that perceives the invisible—an extension of our soul, bridging the gap between the physical world and the spiritual realm.

The psychic mind works in harmony with our conscious mind, yet it operates on a completely different frequency. The conscious mind is the part of us that navigates the everyday world, making decisions based on logic, past experiences, and external input. It's the mind that plans, thinks critically, and reacts to our physical surroundings. In contrast, the psychic mind does not rely on reason or physical evidence. Instead, it receives information from a much higher source—our soul's deeper wisdom, and the energies that surround us. It is not bound by time or space, and it allows us to tap into information that our conscious mind cannot access. This is why sometimes, when we experience something beyond our understanding, it can feel both familiar and surreal—our conscious mind struggles to comprehend it, but our psychic mind knows the truth.

Psychic perception is often described as an inner knowing or a gut feeling, a sense of understanding that doesn't come from the logical mind. It's a deeper connection to the universe, a glimpse into the hidden forces that guide us. Whether it's the sudden realization that a person you've just met has an energy that doesn't sit right with you or an inexplicable feeling that something is about to happen, your psychic mind is always at work. The more attuned we become to this subtle layer of perception, the more easily we can distinguish between what is real and what is a product of our logical minds.

Intuition is the primary way the psychic mind communicates with us. It's often referred to as a "knowing" that doesn't require external validation. Intuition is the whisper of the soul, guiding us through the noise of everyday life. Unlike rational thought, which relies on facts and evidence, intuition often provides us with a sense of clarity that defies logic. We've all experienced it at one time or another—the strong feeling that something is "off" about a situation, or the sudden knowing that we should take a particular course of action, even if we can't explain why.

This innate ability is present in everyone, though not all of us are conscious of it. Some people may dismiss it as a coincidence, while others may chalk it up to random thoughts. But in truth, intuition is the soul's language, a way for us to access the deeper currents of knowledge that exist beyond the physical world. Many times, we overlook or ignore our intuitive feelings, only to regret it later when things don't unfold the way we expected. But intuition is never wrong; it is the most direct communication from our higher selves, telling us exactly what we need to know.

In everyday life, intuition manifests in a multitude of ways. It might show up as a gut feeling, a flash of insight, or an inner knowing that leads us to make decisions that seem to come out of nowhere. You might find yourself thinking about a friend and then receiving a message from them moments later, or sensing when a situation is about to turn bad long before it happens. These small, seemingly random moments are actually your intuition at work. It's like a constant thread of energy connecting you to the greater whole of existence, guiding you through life's twists and turns.

But how do you strengthen your intuition? How do you sharpen this subtle, often overlooked sense so that you can trust it more fully? The answer lies in practice, trust, and openness. Just like any other skill, intuition can be developed and fine-tuned. It begins with being open to the possibility that there is more to the world than what we see with our physical eyes. This openness allows us to connect with the energies that are always around us but often hidden from our awareness.

One of the best ways to strengthen your intuition is through regular mindfulness and meditation. These practices quiet the mind and create space for your psychic perceptions to surface. In a meditative state, you become more attuned to the subtle energies around you, and you begin to receive messages from your higher self. Start by focusing on your breath, clearing your mind of distractions, and allowing yourself to become fully present in the moment. As you sit in stillness, pay attention to any thoughts, feelings, or images that arise. Over time, you'll begin to recognize the difference between your conscious mind's chatter and the quiet whispers of your intuition.

Another powerful exercise is to practice "tuning in" to your intuitive feelings throughout the day. Start by asking questions—whether simple or complex—and notice what pops into your mind. It could be a sense of direction, an image, or a word that resonates with you. Trust the first thought that comes to you, as this is often the voice of your intuition. The more you practice this, the more confident you will become in your intuitive abilities.

Above all, strengthening your intuition requires trust. You must learn to trust yourself, to trust the messages you receive, and to trust the process of allowing your psychic mind to guide you. When you listen to your intuition and follow its guidance, you will begin to see the undeniable results in your life. Doors will open, opportunities will arise, and the path ahead will become clearer. As you continue to nurture this connection, you will feel more confident in navigating the world with a deeper understanding and awareness.

Your intuition is one of the most powerful tools you possess. It is the bridge between your conscious mind and the vast, unseen world that surrounds us. By tapping into your intuitive abilities and learning to trust them, you align yourself with the hidden forces of the universe—those same forces that have been guiding you all along, waiting for you to listen. The more you embrace your intuition, the more you will understand how deeply it connects you to the wisdom of the universe.

In the end, intuition isn't just a gift—it's an awakening. An awakening to the reality that you are far more than the physical body you inhabit. You are a spiritual being, connected to an infinite source of knowledge and wisdom. And by strengthening your intuition, you will discover a deeper sense of purpose, clarity, and empowerment than you ever thought possible.

Trust your intuition, for it is the language of your soul, speaking to you from the vast unknown. The journey to awakening your psychic mind begins with this simple truth: you already know more than you think.

CHAPTER 3

The Mystical Powers of Karma

Karma is one of the most powerful, yet often misunderstood forces in our lives. It is the universal law of cause and effect, governing the way our actions ripple through time and shape the events of our lives. Simply put, karma means that everything we do, say, or think sends out an energy into the universe, and that energy eventually returns to us. This isn't just about good deeds being rewarded and bad deeds being punished, as many may assume. Instead, karma is the natural consequence of every choice, every action, and every thought that we create. It's the unfolding of the law of balance, where we are each given the opportunity to experience the results of our actions in the most fitting way possible.

Karma does not judge. It does not punish or reward. It simply reflects the energy we put into the world. If we act with kindness, that energy will return to us in the form of goodwill. If we act with malice, the universe responds in kind, ensuring that we experience the consequences of those actions. In this way, karma shapes the events of our lives—whether it's through relationships, career opportunities, or the way we feel about ourselves and the world around us. Our present circumstances are the culmination of past choices, and understanding this connection helps us realize that we hold the power to change our future by choosing differently in the present moment.

Our actions don't just affect the immediate moment. The concept of karma goes beyond the here and now, impacting our past and future lives as well. When we are born, we are not born as blank slates but as souls who carry the energy of all the actions we've taken in our past lives. Each soul enters into this world with unresolved debts, lessons to be learned, and karmic agreements to fulfill. These karmic contracts form the very blueprint of our life's journey. It's through these contracts that we meet specific people, experience specific challenges, and encounter situations that seem tailor-made to help us learn and grow.

Karmic contracts are agreements made between souls before they incarnate into the physical world. These agreements are made to facilitate growth, healing, and learning through the experiences we have with one another. For example, you may have a difficult relationship with someone in your life, and it seems as though this relationship is filled with constant conflict. It can feel as though you are locked in a never-ending cycle of emotional turmoil. This could be the result of a karmic contract that was formed in a past life, where both souls agreed to come together again in this life to resolve unresolved issues. These contracts are often hidden from our conscious minds, but they influence the choices we make, the people we meet, and the challenges we face.

Karma is not limited to the present life; it is carried forward from past lives through the cycle of reincarnation. Reincarnation is the process by which a soul is reborn into a new body after death. Each time we incarnate, we bring with us the karmic baggage from our previous lifetimes. This can manifest as unresolved issues, unfinished lessons, or patterns of behavior that we failed to address in our past lives. Just as we carry the consequences of our actions from one life to the next, we also bring the wisdom we gained, though it is often buried deep within our subconscious.

The challenges we face in our current life are often linked to experiences from past lives. For example, you may struggle with a particular fear or phobia that doesn't have a clear origin in this life, but it may stem from a traumatic event in a past life that was never fully healed. Or perhaps you find yourself repeatedly drawn to certain types of people or situations, even though they don't seem to serve your well-being. These patterns are often a reflection of unresolved karma that we need to work through before we can fully break free.

Breaking free from negative karma requires conscious effort and awareness. We must first acknowledge that the karmic cycles we experience are not accidents but opportunities for growth and healing. Each challenge, each painful moment, is an invitation to transform negative karma into positive energy. To cleanse negative karmic influences, we must work on releasing old patterns, forgiving ourselves and others, and healing the wounds that continue to affect us. Techniques such as meditation, mindfulness, energy healing, and seeking forgiveness are powerful tools in this process. These practices help us clear the emotional and spiritual clutter that binds us to past karma and create space for new, positive experiences to enter our lives.

A key component in breaking free from negative karma is learning to shift our mindset. The thoughts we hold and the beliefs we subscribe to directly impact the way we experience karma. If we believe we are destined to fail or that we are unworthy of love or success, we are reinforcing negative karmic patterns. To break free, we must replace these limiting beliefs with empowering ones. By shifting our perception of ourselves and the world, we can begin to create a new reality—one that is no longer bound by the past but is driven by our current intentions and actions.

It's important to understand that we do not have to carry the weight of past mistakes forever. By consciously choosing to create positive karmic cycles, we can break free from the chains of past negativity.

Each moment offers us a fresh opportunity to choose differently, to act with love and compassion, and to release the past. Through this process of self-awareness and transformation, we not only create a brighter future for ourselves but also contribute to the healing of the collective consciousness.

Karma is not something to fear—it is a tool of personal evolution. By embracing its teachings, we can align ourselves with the natural flow of the universe and step into our true power. Understanding the power of karma allows us to take responsibility for our actions and realize that we have the ability to shape our destiny. The more we learn to work with karma, the more we can create the life we desire—one of abundance, peace, and spiritual growth. Through conscious action and the willingness to change, we can break free from the cycles of negative karma and begin to experience the fruits of positive, transformative energy.

CHAPTER 4

Astral Travel – A Gateway to Other Realms

Astral travel, also known as astral projection, is one of the most profound and mysterious experiences that can open up a gateway to realms beyond the physical world. It is the process in which the consciousness or soul separates from the physical body, allowing the individual to travel freely through various dimensions and planes of existence. This out-of-body experience (OBE) can happen consciously, where the traveler is aware of their departure from the physical body, or it can occur spontaneously during sleep or deep meditation.

Astral travel is not confined to just the realm of mystical experiences or fantasy. It has long been acknowledged by spiritual traditions, including those of ancient Egypt, India, and the Far East. In recent years, modern science and metaphysics have sought to explain the phenomenon, with many researchers proposing that it is a form of expanded consciousness that transcends the limitations of the physical body. While there is still debate over the scientific validity of astral travel, countless individuals have reported having vivid, transformative experiences that have shaped their lives in profound ways. These experiences provide insight into the existence of other realms, dimensions, and spiritual energies, inviting us to rethink the nature of reality itself.

The metaphysical explanation of astral travel revolves around the idea that the physical body is not the only vehicle for the soul. According to many spiritual philosophies, the soul or consciousness exists independently of the body, with its own energy field, or "astral body." This astral body can detach from the physical form and journey to other realms of existence, such as the astral plane, which is thought to be a non-physical dimension that intersects with the physical world but is not bound by its laws. Astral travel allows us to experience a new way of perceiving reality, with the ability to explore both known and unknown territories—whether they are otherworldly landscapes, past-life memories, or even interactions with spiritual entities.

Techniques to Access the Astral Plane

Astral travel may seem daunting at first, but with practice, anyone can learn to project their consciousness and journey to the astral plane. It is important to approach this practice with patience and an open mind, as mastering the skill can take time. Below are some common techniques that individuals use to begin astral travel:

1. **Relaxation and Meditation:** Before attempting astral travel, it is essential to relax

the body and calm the mind. Meditation is a powerful tool for quieting the inner chatter and achieving a deep state of relaxation. Focus on deep breathing, calming the nervous system, and clearing your mind of any distractions. As you enter a meditative state, you will begin to feel your physical body becoming more relaxed and lighter.

2. **Visualization Techniques**: Visualization is one of the most effective ways to initiate astral projection. One popular technique is to imagine yourself floating above your body, as if you were a balloon gently rising into the air. Visualize the sensation of weightlessness, and allow yourself to imagine traveling upward, breaking free from the physical constraints of your body. Some individuals also visualize a rope hanging above them or a ladder to climb, using this imagery to help "pull" themselves into the astral plane.

3. **The Rope Technique**: In this technique, you mentally imagine a rope hanging from the ceiling or sky, reaching toward you. As you relax deeper, you visualize yourself grabbing the rope and climbing upward. This physical action in the mind can trick your astral body into releasing from the physical form and begin the journey into the astral realm.

4. **The Roll-Out Technique**: This technique involves the practice of mentally "rolling" out of your body as if you were rolling over in bed. As you become more relaxed, allow your consciousness to follow the motion of your roll, easing yourself out of the physical body. Once you feel that you have moved past the point of detachment, you can begin to explore the astral plane.

5. **Binaural Beats and Sound Frequencies**: Some practitioners use binaural beats or other sound frequencies to induce an altered state of

consciousness. These audio recordings use specific frequencies to synchronize brainwave activity, allowing for a more effortless and guided astral projection experience.

How to Protect Yourself in the Astral Realm

While astral travel can be a rewarding and enlightening experience, it is essential to approach it with caution, especially for beginners. The astral realm is not a neutral place—it is populated by various energies, some benevolent and some malevolent. As with any journey into the unknown, preparation and protection are key to ensuring a safe and positive experience. Here are a few tips to protect yourself during astral travel:

1. **Setting Intentions**: Before embarking on an astral journey, always set clear intentions for your experience. Ask for protection from higher spiritual beings, such as angels or ascended masters, and focus on your purpose

for the journey. Whether you seek knowledge, healing, or spiritual growth, setting a clear intention can help direct your astral travels and keep you focused.

2. **Calling Upon Protection**: Many experienced astral travelers recommend invoking protective energy before you leave your physical body. This can include visualizing a protective shield of white light surrounding you, or calling upon spiritual guardians or guides to accompany you on your journey. It is important to affirm your safety and well-being throughout the experience.

3. **Grounding After Travel**: After returning from an astral journey, it is essential to ground yourself back into your physical body. This can be done by visualizing roots extending from your body into the earth, or by engaging in physical activities, such as deep breathing, eating, or touching objects in your physical

environment to help re-establish your connection with the material world.

4. **Cleansing and Clearing**: It is also a good idea to cleanse your energy field after an astral journey, especially if you encountered negative energies or entities. This can be done through meditation, energy healing, or smudging with sacred herbs like sage or palo santo. This practice ensures that any lingering negative vibrations are released before you resume daily life.

Experiences from the Astral Plane

The astral plane is a vast and multi-layered realm that holds the potential for limitless exploration. During astral travel, individuals report encountering a wide variety of experiences and beings, each offering valuable insights into the nature of existence, consciousness, and the universe. Some of the most common experiences encountered during astral projection include:

1. **Visiting Other Dimensions**: The astral realm is home to a vast array of dimensions and realities, some of which are closely tied to our physical world, while others exist completely outside of it. Travelers often report experiencing landscapes that defy the laws of physics—floating cities, ancient civilizations, or entirely new realms that challenge the boundaries of imagination. These dimensions may appear as they are at a certain point in time, or as a reflection of the traveler's consciousness or emotions.

2. **Meeting Spiritual Guides and Beings**: One of the most profound experiences in the astral realm is meeting spiritual guides, ancestors, or higher-dimensional beings. These entities may offer wisdom, healing, or guidance that can assist the traveler in their spiritual growth.

Many people have reported receiving life-changing advice from these beings, whether it's about personal relationships, career paths, or spiritual lessons.

3. **Past Life Regression**: Astral travel can also facilitate experiences of past lives, where individuals have vivid memories of their previous incarnations. These experiences may provide insight into recurring patterns in one's current life, as well as unresolved issues that need healing or resolution. Understanding past lives can help individuals break free from karmic cycles and evolve spiritually.

4. **Interacting with the Souls of the Departed**: The astral plane is also home to the souls of those who have passed away. While some souls are at peace, others may be in need of healing or guidance before they move on to higher realms. Astral travelers may encounter deceased loved ones, offering them an opportunity to

resolve unfinished business or simply reconnect with those who have passed.

The Power of Astral Travel for Personal Growth

Astral travel is not merely a tool for spiritual exploration—it is also a powerful means of personal growth. As we journey beyond the physical plane, we gain access to a higher understanding of ourselves and the universe. Through astral travel, we can:

1. **Gain Spiritual Wisdom and Insight**: The astral realms are rich with knowledge that can aid in our personal evolution. Whether it's discovering hidden talents, understanding deeper truths about our soul's purpose, or uncovering the mysteries of the universe, astral travel provides a unique opportunity to expand our consciousness and gain valuable insights.
2. **Heal Emotional and Karmic Wounds**: Astral travel can also serve as a powerful tool for healing. By revisiting past lives or exploring

unresolved emotional traumas, we can begin to release the wounds that continue to affect our present life. Astral travel provides the space for emotional and karmic healing, allowing us to confront our fears, let go of negativity, and reclaim our spiritual power.

3. **Strengthen the Connection to the Higher Self**: The higher self is the divine aspect of our consciousness, the part of us that exists beyond the ego and the physical form. Through astral travel, we can strengthen our connection to the higher self, allowing us to access deeper levels of wisdom, intuition, and guidance.

In conclusion, astral travel is a profound and transformative practice that opens up new realms of understanding and personal growth. Whether you are seeking spiritual enlightenment, emotional healing, or simply a deeper connection to the universe, the astral plane offers endless opportunities for exploration. By practicing astral travel with intention, protection, and mindfulness, you can embark on a journey of self-discovery that will forever change the way you experience reality.

CHAPTER 5

The Hidden Forces That Shape Our Lives

Invisible energies are constantly at work in our lives, shaping our experiences in ways we may not fully understand. These forces are not always visible to the naked eye, but they are felt through subtle nudges, synchronicities, and intuitive feelings. These unseen energies can manifest in a variety of ways—from the choices we make to the people we meet and the events that unfold in our lives. Everything in the universe is connected by an energetic flow that influences us at a deep level. These energies are like invisible threads weaving through the fabric of existence, guiding us toward our life's purpose and helping us navigate the challenges we face.

Our thoughts, feelings, and actions are all forms of energy that interact with the universal energy flow. Just as physical energy moves through wires to power machines, the energy we project into the world has a ripple effect. It impacts not only our own lives but also the lives of those around us. This dynamic exchange of energy forms the basis of our relationships, life events, and even our personal growth. When we align ourselves with positive energies, we attract positive outcomes. Conversely, when we are out of sync with our true selves or blocked by negative energies, we may struggle to find balance or fulfillment. Recognizing the hidden forces at play can help us take control of our energy, shifting it in ways that serve our highest good.

How to Tune Into Your 'Home Frequency'

Every individual has a unique energy frequency, a vibration that aligns with their true spiritual self. This frequency is what we call our "home frequency." When we are in tune with our home frequency, we feel a sense of peace, purpose, and alignment with the universe. This is the state where everything flows effortlessly, where our desires begin to manifest, and where we feel most connected to the divine.

Aligning with your home frequency requires awareness and intentionality. It's about stripping away the distractions, the societal pressures, and the noise of everyday life to reconnect with the core of who you truly are. It involves tuning in to the subtle vibrations of your soul, recognizing your deepest desires, and understanding your true purpose. When you align with this frequency, you are not simply reacting to life's circumstances—you are consciously co-creating your reality.

Here are a few practical exercises to help you tune into your home frequency:

1. **Meditation and Stillness**: One of the best ways to tune into your home frequency is through meditation. Find a quiet space, close your eyes, and focus on your breath. As you breathe deeply, let go of any thoughts or distractions. Gradually, you will begin to feel the subtle vibrations of your true self. Listen to what arises in the silence. Your soul will speak to you in the stillness.
2. **Visualization**: Visualizing your desired reality is a powerful way to attune yourself to your home frequency. Imagine yourself living the life you desire—whether it's a fulfilling career, harmonious relationships, or personal peace. As you visualize, feel the emotions of success, happiness, and satisfaction. This exercise helps to create the energetic alignment necessary for manifestation.

3. **Self-Reflection and Journaling**: Take time to reflect on your life's purpose and your core values. What brings you joy? What are your passions? Write down your thoughts in a journal and review them regularly. By identifying what truly resonates with your soul, you can begin to align your actions with your higher self.

4. **Nature Connection**: Spending time in nature is an excellent way to recalibrate your energy. Whether you're walking barefoot on the earth, sitting near a body of water, or simply observing the natural world, nature has a way of restoring balance and helping us reconnect with our true frequency.

When you make the effort to align with your home frequency, you tap into a powerful source of energy that can help you manifest your desires, attract the right people into your life, and navigate challenges with grace and clarity.

The Role of Spirit Guides and Ancestors

Throughout our lives, we are not alone. Whether we realize it or not, we are always supported and guided by spiritual entities—such as ancestors and spirit guides—who are deeply connected to us. These unseen forces offer wisdom, protection, and insight, helping us navigate life's challenges and make decisions that align with our soul's purpose. Spirit guides are often benevolent beings that offer guidance from higher realms, while ancestors carry the wisdom of generations past, offering advice and protection.

Our ancestors are not just part of our past—they are present with us, influencing our choices and experiences. Many cultures believe that our ancestors continue to watch over us, helping us heal unresolved karmic issues and guiding us toward fulfilling our soul's mission. By acknowledging their presence and honoring their wisdom, we invite their assistance into our lives.

Spirit guides, on the other hand, may be beings who have never been human but are deeply connected to our soul's journey. These guides are often assigned to us before birth, tasked with helping us navigate key life lessons. Some people may have one primary guide, while others may have a group of guides who assist them in different areas of their lives. These guides communicate with us in various ways, including through dreams, intuition, signs, and synchronicities.

Here are a few personal stories of how spirit guides and ancestors have influenced lives:

1. **The Healing of Unresolved Trauma**: One person recalls how they began to receive signs from an ancestor after they started exploring their family history. The signs came in the form of dreams and vivid memories, leading them to

uncover unresolved emotional trauma. By acknowledging the guidance, they were able to heal wounds that had affected their relationships and personal growth.

2. **A Sudden Change in Career**: Another individual shares how they felt compelled to change their career path after experiencing a series of strange coincidences. They later discovered that their spirit guide had been nudging them toward a more fulfilling profession, one that would allow them to serve others and follow their soul's calling.

3. **Guidance During a Difficult Time**: In a time of crisis, a person recalls feeling a deep sense of comfort and guidance from a deceased loved one. Through a series of signs and messages, they were able to make a crucial decision that set them on a new path—one that ultimately led to a better life.

By embracing the guidance of spirit guides and ancestors, we can gain clarity, make empowered choices, and navigate life's challenges with confidence.

Grounding and Protecting Your Energy

As we explore the unseen forces that shape our lives, it is essential to recognize the importance of protecting and maintaining our own energy. Our energetic fields are constantly interacting with the world around us, and just as we are influenced by external energies, we also radiate our own. Grounding is a technique that helps us stay centered, balanced, and protected in a world that is often chaotic and draining.

Grounding helps us reconnect with the earth's energy, which serves as a stabilizing force. When we ground ourselves, we anchor our energy in the present moment, allowing us to remain calm and focused. Grounding also helps us release negative energies, such as stress, anxiety, and fear, which can accumulate throughout the day.

Here are a few grounding techniques to help maintain balance and protect your energy:

1. **Walking Barefoot on the Earth**: One of the simplest ways to ground yourself is by walking barefoot on natural surfaces such as grass, sand, or soil. This direct connection with the earth allows energy to flow freely between you and the planet, helping to release tension and restore balance.
2. **Visualization of Rooting**: Sit comfortably with your feet flat on the ground. Close your eyes and visualize roots growing from the soles of your feet, extending deep into the earth. Imagine these roots absorbing grounding energy from the earth, filling your body with a sense of calm and stability.

3. **Breathing Exercises**: Focused breathing exercises can help bring your energy back into alignment. Breathe deeply and slowly, visualizing your breath as a wave that flows through your body, bringing fresh energy while releasing negativity. With each exhale, imagine sending your unwanted energy down into the earth for transmutation.
4. **Energy Shielding**: To protect your energy, visualize a shield of light surrounding your body. This protective shield acts as a barrier, preventing negative energies from affecting you while allowing positive energies to flow freely. You can visualize this shield as a bubble of light, a reflective surface, or even a protective cloak—whatever resonates with you.

By grounding yourself regularly and protecting your energy, you can maintain balance, stay centered, and fully embrace the power of the unseen forces that influence your life.

In conclusion, the hidden forces that shape our lives are both powerful and mysterious. By tuning into our true frequency, honoring the guidance of spirit guides and ancestors, and protecting our energy, we can navigate life with greater ease and clarity. These practices allow us to stay aligned with our highest purpose, creating a life that is fulfilling, balanced, and spiritually enriching. The key is to recognize that these forces are not separate from us—they are part of us, and by working in harmony with them, we can unlock our fullest potential.

CHAPTER 6

Facing the Dark Forces – Protection from Negative Entities

In the realm of spiritual energies, not all forces are benevolent. While there are many positive, supportive, and healing energies that surround us, there are also lower vibrational entities that exist at the opposite end of the spectrum. These entities are often associated with darkness, negativity, and harmful influences. Their impact can range from subtle, invisible shifts in mood or behavior to more overt disturbances that create chaos and fear in the lives of those they affect. These dark forces, operating at a lower frequency, thrive on negative emotions such as fear, anger, hatred, and despair, and they often seek to attach themselves to individuals who are in a weakened or vulnerable state.

Lower vibrational entities come in many forms, from simple thought-forms to more complex and persistent beings. These entities may be the result of negative energy built up over time or they may be attracted to specific situations, such as unresolved trauma or emotional turmoil. They often exploit areas of weakness in our emotional or spiritual state, feeding on our fears, doubts, and insecurities. While their influence can be subtle, over time, they can manifest in physical, emotional, and mental disturbances, including anxiety, depression, illness, and even psychic attacks.

How These Entities Attach to Individuals

The attachment of lower vibrational entities often begins with a breach in the individual's energetic field. This breach can be caused by various factors, such as emotional trauma, substance abuse, or prolonged exposure to negative environments. Once an individual's energy is weakened or out of balance, these entities can find a foothold, attaching to the person's aura and energy field. In this state, they begin to drain the individual's energy, intensifying negative emotions, and sometimes causing dis-ease or depression.

Entities can also attach to physical objects or locations, such as old houses or inherited items. These objects may carry residual negative energy that acts as a magnet for lower vibrational entities. In such cases, the negative energy surrounding the item or location can extend to those who come into contact with it, perpetuating a cycle of darkness and harm.

Protecting Yourself from Negative Energies

While these dark forces are real, the good news is that we are not helpless against them. There are various methods and practices that can help shield us from psychic attacks and protect our energy from the influence of negative entities. Protection begins with an understanding that we are powerful, sovereign beings capable of maintaining our energetic boundaries.

Here are some practical steps to protect yourself from negative energies:

1. **Create Protective Energy Shields**: One of the most effective ways to protect yourself is by visualizing a protective shield around your body. This shield acts as a barrier, allowing only positive energies to enter while blocking out harmful ones. Imagine a bubble of white light surrounding you, or a force field that is impenetrable to darkness. This shield should be reinforced daily to ensure that your energetic boundaries remain strong.
2. **Grounding and Centering Practices**: Grounding your energy is an essential part of protection. By connecting with the earth's

energy, you can stabilize your energy field and create a solid foundation that is difficult for negative entities to penetrate. Try walking barefoot on the earth, practicing deep breathing, or visualizing roots growing from your feet into the ground. This practice helps you stay centered and balanced, making it harder for dark forces to manipulate or attack you.

3. **Protective Visualization Techniques**: Visualizing light is a powerful tool for protecting yourself. Imagine a bright, radiant light surrounding you, forming a protective bubble or cloak. This light can be infused with specific intentions, such as protection, healing, or strength. You can also visualize a mirror on the outside of your energy field that reflects back any negative energy or psychic attacks.

4. **Spiritual Cleansing and Purification**: Regular spiritual cleansing practices are essential for

clearing away negative energy from your aura. Burning sage, palo santo, or other sacred herbs, using sound healing tools like bells or singing bowls, or immersing yourself in salt baths are all effective ways to purify your energy. These practices help remove stagnant or negative energy that may attract dark entities.

5. **Setting Intentions for Protection**: Intention is a key element in spiritual protection. Set clear intentions each day for your protection. This can be done through prayer, affirmations, or simply by stating your desire to remain safe and protected from negative influences. By doing so, you are actively inviting positive energy into your life while rejecting darkness and harm.

The Role of Lightworkers in Battling Darkness

In the battle between light and darkness, lightworkers play a crucial role. Lightworkers are individuals who feel called to work with the divine energy of light, love, and healing in order to uplift others and dispel negativity. Whether they are healers, spiritual practitioners, or simply those who walk the path of service to others, lightworkers are a vital force in helping to protect individuals from lower vibrational entities and dark forces.

Lightworkers are often intuitively drawn to this work because they possess a deep spiritual sensitivity to energy. They have the ability to see, feel, or sense the presence of negative entities, and they use their knowledge of energy work to bring healing and protection to others. This can include everything from conducting energy healing sessions to performing energy clearing rituals or simply offering guidance and support to those who are struggling with negative influences.

The work of a lightworker goes beyond just protecting individuals from negative forces; it involves helping to heal the emotional, mental, and spiritual wounds that allow dark forces to take hold in the first place. Lightworkers assist individuals in understanding their own power, helping them to regain their strength and clarity in the face of adversity. Through their work, lightworkers help others find peace, balance, and healing, ensuring that the forces of darkness are dispelled and replaced with light.

There are also times when lightworkers come together as a collective to combat larger-scale darkness, such as when there is a global crisis or widespread negativity. In these instances, lightworkers may engage in group meditations, collective prayers, or energy healing practices aimed at shifting the collective consciousness toward positivity and healing.

Through their work, lightworkers provide not only protection but also hope, healing, and guidance to those in need. They are the keepers of light, acting as beacons of love and support in a world that often feels overshadowed by darkness. Their mission is clear: to protect, to heal, and to guide others toward the light, ensuring that the forces of darkness do not prevail.

In the end, the battle between light and darkness is not one that we fight alone. By using the protective techniques outlined here, tuning into the help of lightworkers and spirit guides, and strengthening our own energy, we can maintain our sovereignty and power. We can shield ourselves from negative forces, banish darkness from our lives, and live in alignment with the highest energies of love, light, and positivity. The key is to recognize our own divine strength and trust in our ability to create a life that is not influenced by dark forces, but guided by the light within us.

Jack Michael

CHAPTER 7

Transforming Your Life with Mystical Knowledge

In the realm of spiritual energies, not all forces are benevolent. While there are many positive, supportive, and healing energies that surround us, there are also lower vibrational entities that exist at the opposite end of the spectrum. These entities are often associated with darkness, negativity, and harmful influences. Their impact can range from subtle, invisible shifts in mood or behavior to more overt disturbances that create chaos and fear in the lives of those they affect. These dark forces, operating at a lower frequency, thrive on negative emotions such as fear, anger, hatred, and despair, and they often seek to attach themselves to individuals who are in a weakened or vulnerable state.

Lower vibrational entities come in many forms, from simple thought-forms to more complex and persistent beings. These entities may be the result of negative energy built up over time or they may be attracted to specific situations, such as unresolved trauma or emotional turmoil. They often exploit areas of weakness in our emotional or spiritual state, feeding on our fears, doubts, and insecurities. While their influence can be subtle, over time, they can manifest in physical, emotional, and mental disturbances, including anxiety, depression, illness, and even psychic attacks.

How These Entities Attach to Individuals

The attachment of lower vibrational entities often begins with a breach in the individual's energetic field. This breach can be caused by various factors, such as emotional trauma, substance abuse, or prolonged exposure to negative environments. Once an individual's energy is weakened or out of balance, these entities can find a foothold, attaching to the person's aura and energy field. In this state, they begin to drain the individual's energy, intensifying negative emotions, and sometimes causing dis-ease or depression.

Entities can also attach to physical objects or locations, such as old houses or inherited items. These objects may carry residual negative energy that acts as a magnet for lower vibrational entities. In such cases, the negative energy surrounding the item or location can extend to those who come into contact with it, perpetuating a cycle of darkness and harm.

Protecting Yourself from Negative Energies

While these dark forces are real, the good news is that we are not helpless against them. There are various methods and practices that can help shield us from psychic attacks and protect our energy from the influence of negative entities. Protection begins with an understanding that we are powerful, sovereign beings capable of maintaining our energetic boundaries.

Here are some practical steps to protect yourself from negative energies:

1. **Create Protective Energy Shields**: One of the most effective ways to protect yourself is by visualizing a protective shield around your body. This shield acts as a barrier, allowing only positive energies to enter while blocking out harmful ones. Imagine a bubble of white light surrounding you, or a force field that is impenetrable to darkness. This shield should be reinforced daily to ensure that your energetic boundaries remain strong.
2. **Grounding and Centering Practices**: Grounding your energy is an essential part of

protection. By connecting with the earth's energy, you can stabilize your energy field and create a solid foundation that is difficult for negative entities to penetrate. Try walking barefoot on the earth, practicing deep breathing, or visualizing roots growing from your feet into the ground. This practice helps you stay centered and balanced, making it harder for dark forces to manipulate or attack you.

3. **Protective Visualization Techniques**: Visualizing light is a powerful tool for protecting yourself. Imagine a bright, radiant light surrounding you, forming a protective bubble or cloak. This light can be infused with specific intentions, such as protection, healing, or strength. You can also visualize a mirror on the outside of your energy field that reflects back any negative energy or psychic attacks.

4. **Spiritual Cleansing and Purification**: Regular spiritual cleansing practices are essential for clearing away negative energy from your aura. Burning sage, palo santo, or other sacred herbs, using sound healing tools like bells or singing bowls, or immersing yourself in salt baths are all effective ways to purify your energy. These practices help remove stagnant or negative energy that may attract dark entities.

5. **Setting Intentions for Protection**: Intention is a key element in spiritual protection. Set clear intentions each day for your protection. This can be done through prayer, affirmations, or simply by stating your desire to remain safe and protected from negative influences. By doing so, you are actively inviting positive energy into your life while rejecting darkness and harm.

The Role of Lightworkers in Battling Darkness

In the battle between light and darkness, lightworkers play a crucial role. Lightworkers are individuals who feel called to work with the divine energy of light, love, and healing in order to uplift others and dispel negativity. Whether they are healers, spiritual practitioners, or simply those who walk the path of service to others, lightworkers are a vital force in helping to protect individuals from lower vibrational entities and dark forces.

Lightworkers are often intuitively drawn to this work because they possess a deep spiritual sensitivity to energy. They have the ability to see, feel, or sense the presence of negative entities, and they use their knowledge of energy work to bring healing and protection to others. This can include everything from conducting energy healing sessions to performing energy clearing rituals or simply offering guidance and support to those who are struggling with negative influences.

The work of a lightworker goes beyond just protecting individuals from negative forces; it involves helping to heal the emotional, mental, and spiritual wounds that allow dark forces to take hold in the first place. Lightworkers assist individuals in understanding their own power, helping them to regain their strength and clarity in the face of adversity. Through their work, lightworkers help others find peace, balance, and healing, ensuring that the forces of darkness are dispelled and replaced with light.

There are also times when lightworkers come together as a collective to combat larger-scale darkness, such as when there is a global crisis or widespread negativity. In these instances, lightworkers may engage in group meditations, collective prayers, or energy healing practices aimed at shifting the collective consciousness toward positivity and healing.

Through their work, lightworkers provide not only protection but also hope, healing, and guidance to those in need. They are the keepers of light, acting as beacons of love and support in a world that often feels overshadowed by darkness. Their mission is clear: to protect, to heal, and to guide others toward the light, ensuring that the forces of darkness do not prevail.

In the end, the battle between light and darkness is not one that we fight alone. By using the protective techniques outlined here, tuning into the help of lightworkers and spirit guides, and strengthening our own energy, we can maintain our sovereignty and power. We can shield ourselves from negative forces, banish darkness from our lives, and live in alignment with the highest energies of love, light, and positivity. The key is to recognize our own divine strength and trust in our ability to create a life that is not influenced by dark forces, but guided by the light within us.

4o mini

You said:

Chapter 7: Transforming Your Life with Mystical Knowledge • How Intuition, Karma, and Astral Travel Can Change Your Life o Real-life stories or examples of transformation through understanding these forces. o How tapping into these mystical powers can lead to profound personal growth. • Manifesting Your Desired Reality o The connection between psychic abilities and the law of manifestation. o Techniques for manifesting goals by aligning with universal energies. • Living a Higher Vibrational Life o How to raise your vibrational frequency to attract more positivity and spiritual growth. o The importance of daily practices, such as meditation, gratitude, and energy work.

ChatGPT said:

Transforming your life through mystical knowledge requires a deep understanding of the forces at play in the unseen realms. When we open ourselves to the power of intuition, karma, and astral travel, we unlock the potential to experience profound personal growth, healing, and transformation. These mystical forces are not just abstract concepts; they are practical tools that can be harnessed to shape the reality we live in, guiding us toward a life of fulfillment, peace, and spiritual alignment.

How Intuition, Karma, and Astral Travel Can Change Your Life

Real-life stories of transformation often begin with a moment of awakening—a time when a person becomes aware of the unseen energies guiding their path. Take, for example, the story of a woman who had been struggling with recurring financial difficulties. No matter how hard she worked, she found herself stuck in a cycle of debt and stress. Through developing her intuition, she began to recognize the limiting beliefs and emotional blockages that were contributing to her financial struggles. She learned to use her psychic abilities to connect with the energy of abundance, and through conscious manifestation, she started to align her thoughts and actions with prosperity.

As she delved deeper into understanding karma, she realized that her past-life experiences and unresolved karmic debts were playing a role in her current financial struggles. With this awareness, she took steps to heal these past-life wounds and clear negative karmic patterns. Over time, her situation transformed, not through sheer effort, but through aligning her energy with the laws of the universe. The shift in her vibration and understanding of the spiritual forces at play led to new opportunities, unexpected windfalls, and a more empowered, prosperous life.

Another example comes from a man who had been facing constant conflict in his personal relationships.

His family relationships were strained, and he struggled with feelings of resentment and frustration. Through practicing astral travel, he was able to gain clarity about the roots of these conflicts. During his astral journeys, he revisited past lives where he had unresolved emotional wounds with family members. In these other dimensions, he was able to communicate with the souls of his relatives, understanding their perspectives and offering forgiveness. This experience led to healing and a deeper understanding of the karmic contracts that had been affecting his relationships in the present.

Through these stories, we see that by tapping into the mystical powers of intuition, karma, and astral travel, we can bring about profound transformation in our lives. These tools allow us to shed old patterns, heal past wounds, and align with the universe's energies to create the life we desire.

Manifesting Your Desired Reality

Manifestation is the process of bringing our desires into reality by aligning our thoughts, emotions, and actions with universal energies. This connection between psychic abilities and the law of manifestation is not just about wishful thinking; it's about consciously working with the flow of energy that surrounds us. When we tap into our intuitive senses, we begin to understand the subtle energies that influence our lives. We can use these abilities to visualize our desired reality and bring it into being with focused intention.

The first step in manifestation is understanding that we are already connected to the universe's abundant energy. The universe is constantly flowing with opportunities, wealth, health, and love—everything we need to live a fulfilling life is already available to us. The challenge lies in aligning our energy with the flow of abundance. This is where psychic abilities, such as intuition and energy work, come into play. By honing these abilities, we can tune into the vibrations of our desires, strengthen our connection to universal energy, and manifest our dreams into reality.

One powerful technique for manifestation is visualization. When you visualize your goals, you are sending a clear message to the universe about what you want to create. The key is to feel the emotion associated with your desires. For example, if you want to manifest a new job, imagine the excitement, fulfillment, and satisfaction you would feel in that role. Feel the energy of your success, and trust that the universe is aligning to bring that vision into fruition.

Another technique is the practice of gratitude. Gratitude raises your vibrational frequency and opens the door for more blessings to flow into your life. By expressing gratitude for what you already have, you signal to the universe that you are ready to receive more. As you cultivate a grateful mindset, you create a magnetic energy that attracts positive experiences, people, and opportunities into your life.

CHAPTER 8

Embracing the Mystical Path

The mystical path is not one of certainty or ease, but it is one that leads to a deeper understanding of ourselves and the universe around us. To step into the spiritual realm is to open yourself to new dimensions of reality, where every experience is an opportunity for growth, learning, and connection. The journey is not just about discovering hidden truths, but about embracing the unknown with a sense of curiosity and trust. The unseen world beckons, and as you take the first steps toward it, you will find that the path is both profound and transformative.

The Journey Ahead: An Invitation to Explore

As you stand at the threshold of this mystical exploration, remember that the journey is uniquely yours. The spiritual realm is vast and mysterious, and it can offer wisdom and insights that transcend the limitations of the physical world. It invites you to explore beyond what you can see with your eyes, to connect with the unseen energies that shape your life and the universe. The beauty of this journey lies in its infinite possibilities.

Embracing psychic abilities, karma, and astral travel may seem daunting at first, but the rewards are profound. When we begin to develop our intuition, we unlock a deeper connection with our inner selves, our true essence. As we understand karma, we gain insight into the patterns of our lives and how past actions shape our present reality. Astral travel offers us the opportunity to explore other realms, to learn from the higher planes of existence, and to tap into knowledge that would otherwise be inaccessible.

These mystical tools are not just for the gifted few; they are accessible to anyone who is willing to open their mind and heart. By tapping into these hidden forces, you can begin to navigate your life with greater clarity, purpose, and alignment. You will learn to make decisions from a place of wisdom, to release negative patterns, and to manifest the life you truly desire. As you continue to explore these realms, you will find that life becomes richer and more fulfilling—an adventure that goes far beyond the material world.

Practical Tips for Living with an Open Mind

When embarking on a journey into the mystical and spiritual realms, one of the most important things to cultivate is an open mind. The mind is a powerful tool, but it can also be a barrier if we are not willing to embrace the unknown. Too often, we cling to the belief that everything must be rational, logical, and within the confines of our understanding. Yet, the mystical path requires us to let go of these limitations and embrace the mysteries of the universe.

To begin with, it is essential to cultivate a sense of curiosity. Approach the spiritual realm with the wonder and openness of a child, eager to learn and explore. Allow yourself to be guided by your intuition, and trust that the answers you seek will come when the time is right. The path may not always be clear, and you may encounter doubts along the way. However, it is important to remember that every experience is a lesson, and the universe has a way of guiding us toward the answers we need.

Overcoming skepticism is one of the most common challenges on this journey. It's natural to question things that are outside of our everyday experience, and skepticism can be a healthy way to ensure we don't fall prey to false beliefs. However, it is important to recognize that skepticism can also act as a barrier to growth. If we remain rigid in our skepticism, we close ourselves off from new possibilities. Instead, try to approach these mystical practices with an open heart, without judgment or expectation. Allow yourself the freedom to explore, knowing that your experiences are valid, no matter how unconventional they may seem.

A helpful tip for embracing the unknown is to start small. You don't need to dive into complex practices or overwhelming spiritual experiences right away. Begin by observing your own thoughts, feelings, and experiences. Start journaling to track your intuitive insights, the synchronicities you notice in your life, and the ways in which your understanding of karma and astral travel begins to evolve. As you gain confidence in your own abilities, you can gradually expand your practice.

It's also crucial to cultivate patience and persistence. The spiritual journey is not a quick fix, nor is it about instant results. It is a lifelong process of growth, self-discovery, and enlightenment. Allow yourself to be patient with the process and trust that with each step you take, you are moving closer to the answers you seek.

Another powerful practice to incorporate into your journey is mindfulness. By being present in each moment, you create space for clarity and awareness. Mindfulness allows you to tune into the subtle energies around you and to connect more deeply with your own inner wisdom. This practice is essential in helping you navigate the challenges of the spiritual path and to remain grounded as you explore new realms.

Finally, find a community of like-minded individuals who are also on the spiritual journey. Whether it's through meditation groups, online forums, or personal connections, being surrounded by people who share your interests and experiences can be incredibly supportive. Sharing your journey with others can help you stay inspired, grounded, and connected as you continue to grow.

In summary, embracing the mystical path requires openness, curiosity, and trust. It asks us to step into the unknown with faith, knowing that every step we take is part of our spiritual growth. By maintaining an open mind, practicing mindfulness, and cultivating patience, you will find yourself more aligned with the universe and the wisdom it offers. The journey ahead is filled with infinite possibilities—each moment an opportunity to learn, grow, and transform. So, take the first step, embrace the unknown, and let the mystical path unfold before you.

CONCLUSION

As we conclude this journey into the hidden forces of the universe, it becomes clear that these mystical energies—intuition, karma, astral travel, and the unseen forces around us—are not merely abstract concepts, but powerful, transformative forces that shape every aspect of our lives. Whether we are aware of them or not, they are at play, guiding our decisions, influencing our relationships, and steering our personal destinies. The more we come to understand these forces, the more we align ourselves with the greater cosmic flow, unlocking deeper levels of wisdom, insight, and purpose.

The exploration of these mystical forces offers us the opportunity to take control of our lives, to understand the hidden patterns that govern our existence, and to manifest the reality we truly desire. Each force—whether it's the third eye that opens our vision to unseen realms, the karmic laws that bind our actions, or the astral travel that connects us to other dimensions—offers a key to unlock the mysteries of the universe and our own potential. The universe is constantly speaking to us through these forces, and when we open ourselves to their guidance, we begin to see the profound impact they have on our lives.

Final Thoughts on the Hidden Forces of the Universe

These forces are not just esoteric or mystical—they are fundamental to the fabric of existence. They offer us a deeper understanding of our true nature and the interconnectedness of all things. They teach us that we are not merely individuals navigating the world alone; rather, we are all part of a vast, interconnected web of energy that transcends time and space. The more we align ourselves with these energies, the more we can step into our true power, purpose, and potential.

The universe, in all its mystery and majesty, is constantly guiding us toward greater self-awareness and spiritual growth. But it's up to us to recognize and harness the hidden forces at play. Whether it's through tuning into our intuition, cleansing negative karma, or embarking on the journey of astral travel, the universe is offering us endless opportunities to expand our consciousness and transform our lives.

Trusting Your Inner Guidance

Now, it is time for you to take the next step on your own spiritual path. Trust the guidance that lies within you. You possess the innate ability to connect with the unseen realms, to hear the whispers of your soul, and to tune into the deeper truths that govern your life. It's time to trust your intuition, to explore your psychic abilities, and to embrace the spiritual journey that awaits you.

As you step into this world of mystical knowledge, remember that the answers you seek are not outside of you—they lie within. The more you listen to your inner guidance, the more you will come to understand the deeper workings of the universe and your place within it. By trusting yourself and the forces at play around you, you will unlock new dimensions of personal power, growth, and transformation.

The path ahead is yours to discover. The universe has a unique plan for you, a purpose that is waiting to unfold. You are part of a vast, interconnected web of energy and wisdom. Now is the time to step into your true potential, to trust in the hidden forces that shape your destiny, and to explore the spiritual dimensions of your existence. The universe is calling you—are you ready to listen?

Open your heart, trust your soul, and embark on this journey with courage and curiosity. The mystical realms await, and your adventure is just beginning. Embrace it fully, and watch as the forces of the universe guide you to a life of purpose, wisdom, and profound transformation.

Printed in Great Britain
by Amazon